The English Meadow

The English Meadow

A Portrait of Country Life

Yvette Verner

GREEN BOOKS

Published in 2005 by
Green Books Ltd
Foxhole, Dartington, Totnes, Devon TQ9 6EB
edit@greenbooks.co.uk www.greenbooks.co.uk

Design by Rick Lawrence
samskara@onetel.com

Printed in Slovenia on 50% recycled paper

ISBN 1 903998 67 0

Contents

DEDICATION

For Mike, my technological wizard, who has been with me
every flower-strewn (and muddy) step of the way . . . with love

ACKNOWLEDGEMENTS

I am truly grateful to the many people who shared their knowledge of English meadows with me, whether of times gone by, nowadays, or looking ahead to the future. Many are mentioned in this book, but I would also like to thank the following for their kindness:

Joe Costley and Joe Sutton at Plantlife International; Julie Aalen and colleagues at the Weald & Downland Open Air Museum; The British Wildlife Centre; Ruth Roberts and the History Re-enactment Workshop; Joyce Hill of Lawshall for her tales of bygone days; and Michael Alford and Geoff Lincoln for their wonderful black and white photographs, as well as their memories.

Kevan Chambers of Landlife and Donald MacIntyre of Emorsgate Seeds; John le Pla, plus Mark and Deborah Lovill, and Carolyn and Alan Reed for their help; all of the Wildlife Trusts for their kind co-operation; Ditchling Museum, Claas UK Ltd and Massey Ferguson for their technical information; Richard Tomlinson for his photographs of working with wood, plus Plantlife International for photographs of their reserves – expertly taken by Bob Gibbons, Simon Williams and Peter Wilson.

Plus all those kind folk who modestly chose to remain anonymous, and not forgetting Amanda Cuthbert for her patient editing, and John Elford of Green Books, who suggested the idea for this book in the first place.

Introduction

Rarities and everyday flowers mingle happily in meadows.

As recently as the 1950s, England's countryside was full of life, natural beauty and colour. Meadows brimmed with cowslips and cuckoo-flowers, verges were like elongated cottage gardens – overflowing with violets and primroses. Then, with the advent of modern farming, many wildlife species began to disappear. Today, fortunately, public opinion, and government policy, as well as farming, is changing, and more and more species are returning to our meadows.

The *Oxford English Dictionary* defines a meadow as: "A piece of grassland, especially one used for hay." The popular definition is rather more picturesque: "A grassy area containing assorted wild flowers and animals, butterflies, birds and bees." This book is based around both of these descriptions. It gives just a taste of what your local meadows can offer . . . if you take the time to look.

ONE SMALL MEADOW

My husband Mike and I are neither farmers nor landowners. Some ten years ago, however, we were lucky enough to be able to buy an odd half-acre (approx. 40x60 metres) corner of a field. We planted hedges around it, and manage it as a mini-meadow, cutting and removing the hay in late July, then giving it an autumn cut to mimic the grazing that cattle would traditionally have done. Wild flowers have seized their opportunity to settle

Common spotted orchids.

in. Some were there already – others we bought as seeds and sowed onto small patches of earth we had dug over.

Thus it has become a small example of the type of meadow that would once have been common in the countryside, and even now is one of the most likely types to be found in quiet corners. For most of the year, at first glance, it is simply a mixture of small green leaves and grassy shoots. Come warmer weather, however, the meadow awakens.

As the five-bar gate is swung open, cow parsley foams out from the hedgerow shade, its longest stems snapping juicily as you pass. Red campion is a hedgerow-lover too, greeting visitors with stars of bright pink blossom. Fox and badger trails wend their way across the meadow, with snuffle-holes to mark where they found a tasty worm or two.

The sky above is a hazy blue, and a light breeze stirs the flower-filled grasses. Sweet vernal, a traditional meadow grass with a sweet fragrance when mown, pops up early in the meadow year, followed by meadow foxtail, hairy brome and crested dog's tail, plus both rough and smooth meadow-grass.

As a counterpoint to these soft shades of green, wild flowers bloom freely. Buttercups and daisies float above a rich salad of green leaves – each one designed just slightly differently from its neighbours. Meadow diversity contrasts with the strict practicality of a monoculture grass field, like a hand-made rug does when set beside a factory-produced carpet.

Self-heal: a meadow first aid kit.

Tufted vetch runs riot.

Ribwort plantain stands alongside the grass in modest reticence, each bushy brown seed head carrying its own halo of white stamens. Yellow rattle is another unassuming plant, possessing the knack of attaching itself to roots of grasses, thus diminishing them and thereby allowing itself and other species room to bloom. Short green spires carry its hooded yellow flowers, each one destined to create a rattling pod of ripe seeds. Clover blossom, meanwhile, adds ruby splashes of colour nearer ground level, while lofty catsear, with yellow sunburst flowerheads and round-tipped furry leaves, prefers meadows to garden borders – and so does not incur the wrath of gardeners, unlike its dandelion cousins.

Golden cushions of birdsfoot trefoil lie scattered in comfortable repose. Lesser trefoil is more modest in appearance, its clusters of yellow trumpets being so small as to be almost invisible.

The vetch family is well represented. Tufted vetch is one of its most striking members, producing delicate spires of purple blossom that enlist the help of nearby tall grass to reach towards the summer sky.

The twin ruby blooms of common vetch keep each other company on their slender stems. Grass vetchling carries modesty almost to the point of invisibility, with each hair-like stem bearing a single bright red flower, trembling amongst the grasses like a drop of rich wine. Meadow vetchling, on the other hand, is splendidly bold and brassy, holding fire with its blooms until mid-summer, before effervescing amongst the grass with complete abandon.

Then – seemingly popping up overnight – come just a few, common spotted orchids. Their green and purple-blotched leaves clasp a central flower stem, topped by a cone of juicy pink and purple petals – exotic dancers in a field of blossom.

Above all this, waving spires of red sorrel reach towards – and at sunset seem to fuse with – the sky, adding a juicy, vitamin C-packed ingredient to meadow hay.

Pure magic.

(For more on Yvette's meadow, see www.countrymeadow.co.uk)

Hawthorn blossom.

Chapter 1

Meadows of the Past

HISTORIC MEADOWS

MAGNA CARTA 1215

(Runnymede, OS Landranger Map 175, SU 993 733)

Meadows have been the scene of many historic occasions, but one of the most important was the signing of the Magna Carta by King John at Runnymede, beside the River Thames, in 1215. This particular site, which now belongs to the National Trust, may well have been chosen because it was a suitably spacious place for a meeting, and within travelling distance of Windsor Castle, where King John was staying at the time.

There was also a royal precedent for this choice, as Runnymede had served as a meeting place for the Witan Council – Alfred the Great's government. He too had a castle at Windsor, although rather less splendid by comparison. Indeed, the name 'Runnymede' is thought to derive from the Anglo-Saxon words *runieg* meaning 'regular meeting', and *mede* meaning 'meadow'.

The Magna Carta document itself came into being as a result of King John's disastrous attempts to rule Normandy, causing him to apply extortionate taxation throughout England. Thus, in 1215, a group of rebellious English barons rose up against the King and captured the City of London. With the barons grouped in force around him, together with bishops and nobles, King John reluctantly signed the now famous document. An interesting quote from the text is as follows:

"... Wherefore it is our will, and we firmly enjoin, that the English Church is free, and that the men in our kingdom have and hold all the aforesaid liberties, right, and concessions, well and peaceably, freely and quietly, fully and wholly, for themselves and their heirs, of us and our heirs, in all the respects and in all places for ever...."

Another paragraph strikes a somewhat lighter note, but one which women would have particularly appreciated: "... No widow shall be compelled to marry, so long as she prefers to live without a husband...."

The Magna Carta's significance lay not so much in statements of principle and intent, but in establishing an important constitutional principle – that of limiting the power of a monarch by a legal document. Thus were citizens able to begin the road to self-government and justice.

However, this did not happen overnight....

THE BATTLE OF LEWES 1264

(OS Landranger map 198, ref: TQ 396 113)

In the years following the signing of the Magna Carta in 1215, it became clear that King John had little intention of adhering to its terms. His successor, Henry III, was equally unwilling to fulfil his obligations. For despite signing the 'Provisions of Oxford' in 1258 – when he agreed to government of the country by Council, instead of by royal whim – Henry summarily overturned this document in 1261.

When all looked lost for the cause of democracy, however, a bold man of principle, Simon de Montfort – the Earl of Leicester – spoke up for these new ideals and joined with the more liberal barons in opposition to the king. From this conflict, the English Parliament was to be conceived.

The downland slope from which Simon de Montfort led his troops against King John.

A colourful meadow corner.

St. Pancras Priory at Lewes.

So it was that on the 14th May 1264, Simon de Montfort led an army of 4,500 infantry and 500 cavalry to Sussex – to do battle with King Henry III. On that fresh spring morning, the king's headquarters were at St. Pancras Priory at Lewes – beside the River Ouse – while his son, Edward, waited with his forces at the nearby castle. Their combined strength being far greater than that of their challenger, it is likely they were in confident mood.

Simon, meanwhile, gathered his troops on the summit of a downland meadow, between Lewes town and the nearby village of Offham. Many of his soldiers were inexperienced, and must have felt extremely anxious to be set against the king.

Indeed, when the Royal Cavalry charged the left wing, they fled. Prince Edward immediately led his force in hot pursuit of the rebels. This was a mistake, for their opposition scattered and led them away from the scene of battle for two vital hours.

Whilst this was happening, the king and his brother Richard attacked those of Simon's more battle-hardened troops who had remained in position. This action did not go well for them, however. King Henry had two horses killed beneath him, and was "beaten with swords and maces". By the time Prince Edward returned, the battle had been lost. Conditions were agreed for peace, with the king and his son being kept under guard at the castle. During this time, Henry signed an agreement – known as the Mise of Lewes – which was to become a significant step towards greater democracy.

Simon de Montfort used this power to set up the first English Parliament. It was to be attended by two representatives from each chartered borough in the country, plus knights from the shires. Thus those downland meadows had set the scene for increased freedom of the country's citizens.

All did not go smoothly, however. . . .

BATTLE OF EVESHAM 1265

(OS Landranger map 150, SP 037 452)

After the Battle of Lewes, the defeated King John and his son Prince Edward were held captive by Simon de Montfort, who began establishing a more democratic form of government. One fine day, however, Prince Edward was unwisely allowed out on a hunting trip – during which he escaped and fled to join his remaining powerful supporters. Another battle became inevitable.

Simon marched his army boldly towards the opposing troops at Evesham, taking the captive King Henry III with him. On their arrival on 4th of August 1265, however, they found themselves trapped within a loop of the River Avon and vastly outnumbered by the twin armies of Prince Edward and the Earl of Gloucester.

It was a dark and rainy morning. Simon's only hope of success was to slip between the armies of Edward and Gloucester set out before him. He therefore arranged his forces accordingly, and charged.

Although he had some initial success with this tactic, Simon's forces were soon surrounded and overwhelmed. The king's troops pursued their opponents to the last man, cutting them down much as they would have done the meadow grasses which surrounded them, in more peaceful times.

The body of Simon de Montfort was severed into pieces and dispatched to different ends of the country, although his torso was eventually sent to Evesham Abbey, in time becoming a centre for pilgrimage.

This struggle for greater democracy had not been in vain, however, for Parliament had been shown to work.

BATTLEFIELD WILD FLOWERS

Since the carnage of two world wars, poppies have become a widely accepted symbol of the loss of life that inevitably accompanies armed conflict. In medieval days, however, this sadness was symbolised by an entirely different wild flower – purple loosestrife.

Battles often took place in meadows and fields near rivers and streams, which have served to indicate territorial boundaries since time immemorial. This environment is also the chosen home of purple loosestrife. It is indeed possible, therefore, that the upheaval such battles caused had the result of distributing and trampling loosestrife seeds more vigorously into the soil than normal. Thus a bumper crop of these deep red spires of bloom would spring up the following year, as if to remind superstitious folk of where blood had been spilt.

However, everything in nature was perceived to have a practical purpose, so purple loosestrife was also sometimes plucked and placed upon the yoke of fractious oxen, to calm them down.

Purple loosestrife with green-veined white butterfly.

MEADOW HEDGES

"A bundle of sticks and a bank of earth."

Hedges are a wonderful asset to the English countryside, looking so natural that they could almost appear to have planted themselves. So how did they get here, and will they survive into the future?

After the last Ice Age drew to a close some ten thousand years ago, early ground-cover plants began to reappear, creating natural meadows. Where soil was sufficiently thick, primeval forests took over, but glades were still formed by wind-blown trees after fierce storms. These contained small meadows, where creatures such as elk and deer would graze.

Pollen records show that by 4000 BC, ground-cover plants like saxifrage, birdsfoot trefoil, self-heal and oxeye daisies had joined meadow grasses, broadening the available grazing menu.

As time went by and early man began to settle and farm, these meadows and glades were extended. Dartmoor, for instance, still shows signs of Bronze Age field systems from around 2000 BC. In rocky or moorland areas such as this, stones were painstakingly gathered from fields and meadows for use in building walls for their boundaries – a task that took great skill and patience. A boulder too immense to be moved sometimes became the starting point of such a wall. (Interestingly enough, in the West Country, laneside walls are called 'hedges').

Boundaries have always been important. Without them both wild and domesticated animals would have wandered in and out at will. When people started to become farmers, rather than

Hedgerows along a Green Lane.

hunter-gatherers, they hacked out fields from woodland – sometimes leaving strips of trees to mark edges. Even now some of these still form parish boundaries. Earth banks and ditches enclosed many Iron Age settlements, fields and common grazing land around 700 BC, a system that was still in evidence during successive Roman invasions from around 40 AD to 410 AD.

The Romans brought with them knowledge of hedges from other parts of their empire, and during quieter periods of their reign here – after Queen Boudicca was defeated in 61 AD, for instance – some hedges were planted around newly acquired estates.

With the passage of time, these banks, ditches and hedges fell into disrepair. However, the eventual upsurge of the Saxon population meant that the original banks were topped with fresh stakes driven into the ground and interwoven with hazel wands. This formed a difficult 'hurdle to get over' for animals and trespassers alike. Hawthorn, or quickthorn as it is perhaps

more descriptively known, is fast to set roots and grow, but despite this, much of its length would have needed regular replacement.

Meadows set within these secure boundaries would have flourished, aided in no small measure by a particularly useful Roman introduction – the scythe. This tool allowed the harvesting of sufficient hay to keep the best farm animals alive during winter. It also enabled the cutting of fragrant wild herbs, such as lady's bedstraw, for folk to sleep soundly upon during this period of relative peace.

Following their arrival at the Battle of Hastings in 1066, the Normans adapted and improved such hedges as there were around their newly acquired estates, by ordering that the gaps be filled by hawthorn seedlings and bushes. As these were not yet strong enough to confine cattle, the art of hedge-laying was introduced, with main hedgerow stems being cut part-way through and bent sideways. This encouraged thicker growth. Hazel uprights, meanwhile, were inserted to help fill the gaps

A hawthorn hedge in May.

and support interwoven hazel wands across the top, which added strength.

In time, the creation of this thicker linear habitat gave shelter to a wide variety of wild plants such as hedge mustard, hedge bindweed and 'Jack-by-the-hedge' (or garlic mustard). Wild animals too were quick to spot the advantages hedges provided for burrows and hunting – sometimes counter-productive for those at the lower end of the carnivore food chain!

Hedgehogs in particular were very partial to hedges – gaining their name both from this favourite habitat and the noisy relish with which they chew slugs and worms, their favourite foods. Badgers were hedgehogs' main predators. These bumbling black and white animals are equipped with very long digging claws, and can use these sharp tools to unroll hedgehogs for their supper, although worms are easier to catch. Gypsies were reputed to bake hedgehogs in clay over their camp fires. The spines would then peel away with the baked clay, leaving their cooked flesh to form a tasty meal – a more worthwhile fate perhaps than being squashed flat by today's motorised traffic.

Game birds would guide their infant broods amongst the long grass beneath the shelter of hedges, while other birds, such as yellowhammers, wrens and hedge sparrows (also known as dunnocks) gladly took refuge amongst hedge branches. Even today there are more birds' nests per mile in hedgerows than in woodland trees.

Over the centuries, other hedge plants such as blackthorn, dogwood, spindle, and buckthorn – their berries often sown by birds – joined with hawthorn to form flourishing field boundaries. Oak trees and hazel bushes sprang up from acorns and nuts buried by squirrels and jays. Fruit trees, such as apple, pear and plum, were added, to act as a wild larder for locals. Holly bushes were another useful addition, with lopped branches being gathered for decoration at Christmas, or tied to a rope and hauled down a chimney to clean it of soot. Sections of hedge containing holly were traditionally left uncut in some parts of the country, in the belief that these prickly leaves would prevent witches from running along the hedgerows.

Corn and hay were now safely protected from wind, weather and wandering animals. Indeed, the internal temperature of a meadow or field enclosed by hedges, which act as a twiggy kind of thermal vest, is measurably increased.

The Enclosure Acts proclaimed by Parliament, however, disrupted rural life from the sixteenth to the eighteenth century, turning countryside management upside down. Instead of folk being able to let their goat, cow, or geese wander on the common grazing land, commons were enclosed and shut off from general use. Fields, meanwhile, which had

Honeysuckle.

Brambles.

Hawthorn berries.

previously been farmed in strips and held by individual villagers, were now combined to form large fields with one owner. Meadows often suffered the same fate, with the exception of a number of Lammas lands.

Lammas Meadows

For century upon century, important events in the farming year have been linked with religious festivals. Lammas Day is said to derive from the Saxon word *Leffmesse* (meaning 'loaf mass'), the farm harvest celebration. On Lammas Day, 1st August, cattle were allowed back into the meadows to graze the grassy 'aftermath' of hay mowing. Candlemas Day, celebrated on 2nd February, was the date when meadowland was 'shut up for hay' once more and cattle excluded, so that the next crop of meadow hay could grow in peace. Ancient Lammas meadows still follow these customs today.

Even though individual strips of land had been informally swapped for centuries, in order to provide more convenient fields for farming, enclosure inevitably meant hardship for many, who were now forced to seek work on the enlarged farms of those more fortunate. Theoretically, relocation of the dispossessed to new (usually small and inconvenient) plots of land was seen as compensation, but in practice the poor lost out. Parliament's strongest argument, however, was that enclosure increased agricultural productivity, which was indeed the case.

If public footpaths had not been allowed to survive this upheaval, villagers might have found it difficult to reach their work, the village shops or church. For footpaths generally head straight for their objective, while roads often need to take a more roundabout route.

One job for which there was a sharply increased demand, however, was that of the hedger and ditcher, as Parliament decreed that hedges must bound all these new fields.

Using experience gleaned from the past, hawthorn was

Wild rose hips.

chosen to form the thousands of miles of new hedging required to enclose these redesigned farmlands.

Hawthorn berries were collected and sown in special plots, the resulting seedlings being nurtured until they were big enough to transplant to the edges of these enlarged fields. Ironically, the management of these new hedges kept some villagers in work. It must have been hard, though, for a man to plant a hedge which would divide him from what had once been partly his own land.

Over time, these new hedges accommodated a similar variety of hedgerow species to those planted centuries before, although not to such a diverse degree. Indeed, it is now agreed that the way to discover the age of a hedgerow is to pace out a hundred yard (twenty-seven metre) stretch along it. Having counted the number of different hedge plant species found there, repeat this on two or three other sections and then work out the average figure. (Climbers such as honeysuckle and ivy don't count, although wild rose does). If you multiply this result by 100, you have a surprisingly accurate guide to the age of your chosen hedge. Thus a hedge containing an average of four woody species per twenty-seven metre stretch is estimated to be four hundred years old – a venerable habitat indeed, and one which was estimated to be over half-a-million miles long, although not all of it was necessarily that old.

This happy state of affairs for nature and the landscape was not destined to last much longer, however. Following the Second World War, successive governments encouraged hedge removal, with the understandable aim of helping food production. Ever bigger machinery was developed to work in these enlarged fields, which meant that even more hedges were removed to make these machines cost-effective. Meanwhile, there were food surpluses, not shortages.

In some parts of the country, fifty per cent of hedges were grubbed out, and wildlife, which also faced the accompanying threat of pesticides, went into sharp decline. Thankfully there are now national and local government grants for hedge replanting, and little by little restoration is taking place. Meadows in particular seem made for the embrace of sturdy hedgerows. Human beings, too, benefit from hedges in ways that we did not fully realise until they began to disappear.

To walk beside a hedgerow of an early morning, where dewy cobwebs hang from berry-laden branches, and butterflies drowse amongst the honeysuckle, is to keep company with generations before us. Our forebears would have known the best spots within such hedges to collect rose hips for jelly, hazelnuts to store for Christmas, and elderberries to brew a fine wine. We in our turn might well agree that the world seems a better place when it contains thriving country hedgerows.

WATERMILLS AND WINDMILLS

WATERMILLS

Watermills were one of the first inventions to harness natural power. Their initial requirements – nearby fertile land and a reliable source of flowing water – have remained the same over countless centuries. Thus watermills that survive today are likely to be on an ancient site, even though the mechanisms will have changed.

Some watermills are associated with 'floated' watermeadows, whose levels of water were, and in some cases still are, regulated by a system of 'hatches' and drainage channels. These hatches (small locks) were raised or lowered in order to flood one section of meadowland at a time – a system that worked very efficiently when there were sufficient skilled operators (called 'drowners') to work them.

More frequently, though, watermills are to be found beside fast-running water that passes fields and meadows on its route. The gigantic waterwheel, with its wooden paddles, is set into a deep water channel (the millrace). As the flowing water pushes these paddles round, the shaft of the waterwheel connects with a series of vast millstones. These turn the machinery needed to grind corn and produce flour for a multitude of bakery needs.

At the time of the Domesday Book in 1086, there were over five and a half thousand working English watermills. Today they are something of a rarity. Stone or brick-built for strength and water-resistance, these substantial buildings still look at one with their surroundings. Nowadays most are cherished for their historical significance in our forebears' lives, and some are working still.

WINDMILLS

Windmills in England are thought to date from around the 12th century. The earliest of these were called post mills, as the main body of the mill was balanced on a very large upright post, enabling the sails to be turned in the correct direction to catch the wind. These windmills are traditionally painted white, and show up to perfection on the brow of a breeze-blown hill.

A waterwheel of the 17th century.

rumbling, rotating world of the miller, who was once responsible for the flour that makes our daily bread.

Apparently millers were not without their faults, however. A freshwater fish called the bullhead, which lives in rivers and streams, has a head that is disproportionately large for its body. The country nickname for this fish is 'miller's thumb' – as the miller was reputed to press heavily with his thumb on the scales as he weighed out flour to his customers, resulting in less flour for them, but greater profit for the miller.

Smock mills are well named, as they do indeed resemble the traditional countryman's smock. Although the main body of a smock mill resembles a post mill, its white-planked body is fixed to a solid base, which is often painted black. Just the top cap and sails rotate to catch the wind.

Tower mills are built entirely of stone or brick. Although generally unpainted, a tower mill is an impressive sight, as its conical body stretches skywards and the sails go round with a steady 'whoosh, whoosh'.

There have always been some people who are so taken with the attractive design and countryside associations of disused windmills that they buy them to live beside or actually in. One such enthusiast was the poet and historian Hilaire Belloc, who owned Shipley windmill in Sussex from 1906–1953. More recently this windmill has been the fictional home of the television detective Jonathan Creek.

Today, many watermills and windmills are open to the public on a regular basis. Your local library should be able to provide you with details. It's certainly a unique experience, for, as soon as you enter a mill, you are engulfed in the creaking,

This type of mill was named after a traditional countryman's smock.

Yellow waterlilies cover this peaceful mill pond.

FARMHOUSES

An example of a 13th century home.

It would appear that chieftains, lords and their ladies have always lived in greater style than their more modest citizens. Indeed, any innovations in home building could take a century or more to filter down to the general population. So where did the people in the middle – the farmers who owned the meadows – live?

14TH CENTURY

Up until the 14th century, the homes of English farmers had not changed a great deal since the Saxon hut, with its wooden walls and thatched roof with a hole for the smoke to drift out of. The home of an influential farmer did not differ significantly in design from that of his neighbour, although such evidence that remains today is slender. Houses made of flint, however, survive rather better, and a few remaining examples, discovered on the South Downs, have left sufficient clues for us to deduce their construction.

A typical home might measure 10 by 5 metres, with a framework of wooden posts initially filled with wattle and daub (woven twigs plastered with a mixture of mud and cattle dung). Later, however, this in-filling was replaced by a stronger layer made of the rough flints that littered Downland areas. A low roof, thatched with furze or straw and incorporating a smoke-hole, would have topped the resulting cottage. Any window would have been necessarily small, with vertical wooden bars for safety and a wooden shutter to close at night or in bad weather. The wooden door would probably have been left open as much as possible during the day, except during the worst of mid-winter weather.

The beaten earth floor would have had a central hearth area, with cooking pots and earthenware jugs nearby. It is likely that a wooden bench or two would have served as furniture, with bracken or hay for bedding, perhaps covered by a cowhide.

15TH CENTURY

By the early fifteenth century, life in rural England was beginning to feel more secure. 'Cruck'-framed buildings were formed by splitting naturally curved tree trunks into two matching halves. When fixed together at the top, these formed a large arch, which together with neighbouring arched pairs, a horizontal ridge-pole, rafters and lateral tie-beams, enabled the creation of an airier 'open hall' style of housing. There was still a central fireplace, but the construction of a private room at one end of the hall, for the farmer and his wife, was a significant advance.

Bayleaf, a 15th century hall house.

By the end of the fifteenth century, the homes of wealthier farmers had become considerably more sophisticated. They were constructed of stout vertical oak beams with cross-braces; the panels in between being filled with wattle and daub. These rested on the greatest timbers of all, laid flat on the ground to form the 'sill'. The central portion of the building was still an open hall design, but now both ends were partitioned off, with boarding inserted to form ground and first floor rooms. These first floors were often jettied, and, set beneath a clay-tiled roof, they created the traditional style of farmhouse still seen in children's storybooks.

A buttery and pantry (for storing food and utensils) might well have occupied one of these new ground floor areas, with a separate chamber above. The first floor 'solar' room at the other end (reached by a stoutly constructed, fixed-ladder type of staircase) became a bedroom for the farmer, his wife and perhaps their children.

A striking refinement in some of the grander homes was the insertion of a 'garderobe', or built-in toilet, into the bedroom. This was basically a plank with a hole in it set inside a cupboard incorporated into the house jetty, where it overhung an outside pit. This was a far better option than a chamber pot (except for the servant whose job it was to empty the pit with a long-handled scoop).

The ground floor 'parlour' room was useful for storage or extra sleeping space. Family meals, meanwhile, would have been eaten in the central hall, from a table set with pewter mugs, bone-handled knives and wooden 'treen' platters.

16TH CENTURY

This attractive style of building continued throughout the sixteenth century, apart from one major development. The open hearth in the centre (or heart) of the home, was now enclosed within a substantial brick chimney with an inglenook fireplace, and a bread oven to one side. With the smoke thus safely channelled, first floor rooms could also be inserted above the centre of the house, either side of the new chimney. Another useful adaptation was the insertion of wooden staircases, made of triangular oak blocks, instead of simple ladders.

In areas of natural stone, such as the Yorkshire Dales or the Lake District, substantial stone walls formed even stronger buildings, well able to withstand the worst that the weather could throw at them. These farmhouses were long and narrow, with stone barns added at the far end. Roof beams needed to be substantial to bear the weight of stone slabs or tiles; these homes were warm in winter and cool in summer. It is also fair to say, though, that people still needed to wrap up warmly when cold winds whistled round the rooftops, and smoke blew back down the chimneypots.

West Country granite caused particular construction difficulties in Devon and Cornwall. Some farmhouse walls were formed from large granite blocks simply set on top of each

other; others were made of smaller stones or even rubble fixed with mortar. Roofs might be made of slate, with house leeks growing on top, or thatched, with sparrows nesting in the eaves.

Of immense practical assistance in any house, however, was the arrival of glazed windows. Initially thin panels of horn were used, but when glass-paned diamond windows were invented this was a great step forward.

A 17th-century kitchen would have looked much like this.

A 16th-century bedroom garderobe, with a replacement seat.

17TH CENTURY

Although timber-framed buildings still flourished during the seventeenth century, the supply of wood became seriously depleted. Beams were used more sparingly, and in some areas farmhouses were more likely to be built of brick or flint. Their substantial brick chimneys were an integral part of the design, rather than a later addition. Ground flooring was also constructed of brick, and spiral wooden staircases appeared. An important advantage of brick buildings in general, especially as towns grew ever larger, was their resistance to fire.

A present-day timber roof structure. Photo © Richard Tomlinson.

18TH CENTURY

By the eighteenth century, brick and stone farmhouses of elegant design were being built for Georgian farmers. Although not as grand as mansions for well-to-do merchants and noblemen, the impressively pillared front entrance with geometrically matched windows on either side, high roof line and a neat chimney set at each end, sent out a clear message that here was a farmer who had arrived on the social scene.

A mock-up of an 1860s kitchen cupboard.

19TH CENTURY

In the nineteenth century, industrialisation created a wide market for supplying food to the rapidly expanding towns. An equally wide range of architectural styles also found favour in towns, with the Victorian Gothic revival proving most popular. Country tastes, however, were generally more conservative.

20TH CENTURY

The twentieth century heralded many changes in farming methods, brought about in part by the need for greater food production during two world wars. Farmhouse design returned to a more practical, rectangular style. Many farmhouses, however, appeared from the outside to have changed little from when they were originally built. Inside, the many domestic conveniences that modern-day living required brought a new degree of comfort to the farmer and his family – the tradition of a sickly newborn lamb being restored to life by being placed in the bottom oven of the farmhouse kitchen Aga, being a practical example.

21ST CENTURY

In the twenty-first century, farming faces new challenges. However, it still continues to be a twenty-four hour a day job, and a house that welcomes a farmer home – muddy boots and all – must surely mean as much today as it did centuries ago.

FARMWORKERS' COTTAGES

Whilst increasing prosperity brought about a remarkable expansion in the building of farmhouses and homes for the wealthy, accommodation for farm labourers and their families progressed at a far slower rate. So where did the families of the men who mowed the meadows live?

The two chief options for the poor were either to move into the old houses left behind when farmers moved on to more modern houses, or to live in cheaply-built cottages which might come with their job or be rented from landlords.

14TH CENTURY

During the fourteenth century, the poorest of people still lived in a 'hovel' – a word which was at first purely descriptive of a basic shelter with a central fire. As time went by, however, this term implied a pitiful living place, which demonstrates how relatively quickly things began to improve.

15TH CENTURY

By the fifteenth century, most villagers lived in simple beamed cottages with either wattle and daub or flint walls. Basic stone cottages could also be built by a family with traditional knowledge of building field walls and barns, or with the addition of skilled work by artisan stone masons and carpenters.

Failing this, tradition decreed that if a cottage could be erected overnight and have smoke coming out of its chimney in the morning, then it was deemed to be owned by its builder; a feat which could only be achieved by choosing an isolated spot, such as the edge of a common, and secreting a collection of building materials nearby – especially stones for the chimney and a flint to light the fire.

In the south-west of England, however, most farmworkers lived in single-storey cob cottages. Thick, rubble stone walls were built up two feet at a time, covered with a mixture of clay and straw, plus sand or grit, then left to dry. A further two feet section was then added all round, except where timber-framed doors and windows were required, before being left to dry again. This process continued until the eaves were reached, when rafters were erected (partially supported by the chimney), and thatched. The walls were then given two coats of limewash.

There is still a saying in that part of the country, 'Given a good hat and a dry pair of shoes, a cob cottage will last forever.' In many cases, this traditional building method has indeed withstood the test of time.

An old English cottage.
Photo © Bertrand Collet.

Poplar Cottage, built in the 17th century.

16TH CENTURY

Thatched roofs were still popular on simple cottages during the sixteenth century and beyond. The tools required are deceptively basic, but the making of a sound thatch depends on the skill with which they are wielded.

Wheat straw, also known as 'long-straw', was spread on the ground beside a cottage to be re-roofed, dampened with water and then tied in compact bundles, known as yealms or holms. Beginning at the bottom-right-hand corner of the roof, the long-straw was laid out in vertical courses

16th century spinning wheel.

an arm's-stretch across, with the base row being particularly well secured to the rafters with split brambles or tarred cords.

Successive layers were then firmly anchored with bent hazel wands, known as sways, driven deep into the straw beneath. The exposed straw was combed straight with a side-rake. Each time a vertical course was completed, the long ladder was moved to the left and another course laid beside it. Thatching spars (also known as spics or pins) were particularly useful when the thatcher neared the roof ridge. A final row of thick straw yealms was laid thickly over the ridge and secured on both sides by sways and a traditional pattern of cross-pieces or tarred cord. The process is still much the same today.

Norfolk reed has also always been popular for thatched roofs. This reed is longer and stronger than wheat-straw, and is patted into place with a short wooden paddle called a 'leggat'. The finished result costs twice as much, but lasts twice as long and is reputed to repel nesting birds better

The cottages beneath these thatched roofs often had bread-ovens built to one side of the fireplace. Fires of peat, furze or wood were lit within these ovens, then raked out when the temperature was judged to be sufficiently warm, when bread dough in a simple 'cottage loaf' shape would be put in to cook.

Cottage floors were usually made of beaten earth and sometimes given a covering of fresh rushes. A brick floor would have been considered a great advance.

17TH CENTURY

During the seventeenth century, women as well as men were still kept very busy; not only did they work at home, tending their gardens to make herbal medicines and ointments, minding chickens, spinning and weaving, fetching water from the well, cooking, and bringing up children – but they also helped with haymaking and harvest.

Wells were an important source of water.

Working men, meanwhile, could work full-time for a particular local farmer, or hire themselves out for piece-work. In addition to this, they might have a cow or pig to tend, as well as chopping logs for the fire and growing sufficient vegetables to last the family year-round.

Their homes were still of traditional design, many being timber-framed (although with poorer quality timber, now that the woods and forests were being cleared), but further home comforts made their presence felt; boxed in staircases to stop the draughts, for instance, and glazed windows.

18TH CENTURY

By the late eighteenth century, some homes for working folk and their families were clap-boarded – which is to say the framework was covered by overlapping softwood planks. Although lacking somewhat in insulation, this economic system of construction worked well as long as the exterior surfaces were regularly painted to keep out the rain.

Earth-closets were still situated in the gardens, with chamber pots ready for use beneath the beds at night. Hand-made pegged rugs – using short strips of material from worn-out

A washtub, washboard and posser.

clothes, which were pushed through a piece of clean sacking with one 'leg' of a dolly peg – were warm beneath the feet as cottagers undressed. Then they hopped into a bed with a warmed brick wrapped in a scrap of thick material, to act as a hot-water bottle.

19TH CENTURY

During the latter part of the nineteenth century, brick cottages were built for farm workers. Often constructed in semi-detached pairs, they had a 'wash-house' out the back, with a big copper boiler in one section and an outdoor toilet enclosed in the other.

The mangle – a vital piece of equipment on washday.

The wash-tub came complete with a washing-dolly (a small three-legged stool, with a long handle arising from its centre, used to swish clothes around in hot water), or a posser (a long-handled, perforated copper hemisphere, which pummelled clothes and water together). A corrugated wooden washboard, against which stubborn stains were rubbed away, was another necessity.

When things were 'damp-dry' – either from being pegged out on the line or hung from a clothes-rack suspended from the kitchen ceiling – they were smoothed with a flat iron, made of solid cast metal. You really needed two irons on the go: one to be warming by the fire (ready for instant use when the other

A 19th-century clapboard cottage.

A 1916 sampler.

20TH CENTURY

During the course of the twentieth century, newly-built farmworkers' homes improved beyond cottagers' dreams. With indoor sanitation, airy windows, three bedrooms, living room and spacious kitchen, life became a good deal more comfortable. The garden was sizeable, enabling traditional home-grown fruit and vegetables to remain on the menu.

So what of the old farmworkers' cottages that still stood – or leaned – stubbornly at the end of the lane? Surprisingly enough, the Second World War was the saving of many. Council sanitary regulations had often placed these seemingly tumbledown homes top of the list for demolition but, with more important things on their minds, officials were glad to find homes of any kind still standing.

By the end of the war in 1945, the saying: 'If you want to do someone a bad turn, leave them a thatched cottage in your will' no longer rang quite true. People hungered for peace and stability, almost as much as food and drink, and old cottages seem to exude these qualities. True, most young couples sought out modern homes in the towns and cities that were now coming back to life, but by the 1960s sufficient people had decided to live in the country to create a boom in the prices of thatched and beamed, or hand-quarried stone and tile cottages.

So what is it like to live in a place where you have to remember to duck before you come in the back door, hang on tight to the handrail, or rope, as you go up the creaking spiral stairs, and know the knack of pushing at window-corners to get them to open in damp weather?

"It's like being greeted by an old friend every time I come home," says a twenty-first century cottage-dweller. "I'm not looking at everything through rose-tinted spectacles. I remember my great-granny's cottage, where a pump at the gate served as kitchen tap, the earth closet was a long walk up the garden, oil lamps cast shadows of an evening. Yet, despite all that, there was an indefinable atmosphere of peace and stability. I loved it then, and, with the benefit of electricity and modern plumbing, I still do."

iron cooled), plus another one to thump down on the clothes and vanquish the creases. Every time the irons were swapped round, it was important to remember to wipe their smooth metal surface with a rag, to save any smuts being transferred to the clean clothes.

The outdoor water-closet (better known as the WC or 'privvy') usually came with a supply of cut or torn squares of newspaper hung on a handy nail in the wall. This provided the opportunity for a quiet read whilst sitting there, although tantalisingly seldom was an entire article contained on the one piece.

Although healthier than an earth closet, the privvy was a dark and cold place to visit before bedtime. I heard of a girl who had another hazard to overcome – for someone had to go out and hold the family goat before she dared set foot outside the back door. A chamber pot beneath the bed was an easier option, and, a 'stone' glazed pottery hot-water-bottle, to take the chill from the sheets, was a definite boon.

The Victorian style of dark furniture, armchairs with antimacassars (to prevent gentlemen's hair oil from marking the material), plus a potted aspidistra in the corner – lived on for a good while in homes such as these.

COTTAGE GARDENS

No inch of space.

Farmworkers needed cottage gardens to feed their families, especially after the Enclosure Acts of the 16th century, when common land became private. In these circumstances, cottage gardens could make the difference between food on the table and starvation.

Initially, a cottage garden was laid out on a strictly utilitarian basis. Several rectangular beds were dug, enabling the harvesting of crops on a day-to-day basis, with no unnecessary trampling down of nearby fruit or vegetables. Thin grassy pathways grew up between these different types of plots, much as they still do on in vegetable gardens today.

The aim was for there to be food to gather at all times of the year, although some crops – such as parsnips and carrots – could be buried in straw-lined earth pits, or 'clamps', and dug up again when needed.

Potatoes, parsnips, onions, leaf beet, peas and broad beans were mainstay crops, while salad ingredients such as radishes, rocket and lettuce were welcome additions in the spring. Bowls of 'potage' – a soup whose consistency varied with whichever vegetables were available to go in it – appeared with what must, at times, have been monotonous regularity.

The herb garden, which usually occupied the space nearest the cottage, fell within the wife's domain. Borage, comfrey, hyssop, vervaine, mint and marjoram were amongst these plants, valued for their medicinal and culinary properties. Also present, of course, were the four herbs famed as the chorus of that popular folk song 'Are You Going to Scarborough Fair' – parsley, sage, rosemary and thyme.

Meat was a luxury food, and only rarely available to the poor. However, there were 'ways and means' of obtaining some. Wire snares could be set in the hedgerows, at points where a country-dwellers' trained eye could spot regular pathways made by rabbits. A catapult, made from a Y-shaped branch of ash or hazel, with a length of square black elastic plus leather fastenings, was known as 'the poor man's shotgun', and many a country lad could put this to good use.

Anything brought home hidden inside a countryman's jacket (the origin of the phrase 'poacher's pocket') would be skinned or plucked, then cut up and tossed into a pot of vegetables bubbling on the fire or hob. Bones, skin or feathers would be burned or buried, and hopefully no one of importance was any the wiser.

Bread and cheese were also important components of a cottager's staple diet. The traditional cottage loaf – a large cushion of dough with a smaller one on top – was an easy shape to bake because it required no tin. Together with a chunk of cheese and a bottle of tea, the top portion separated from the base could form the mid-day meal for a man hard at work mowing a meadow.

It is one of the more endearing quirks of human nature that we 'make the best of things' when we can. Thus cottage gardeners began to broaden their scope by including wild flowers and plants in their plans. Some would have self-seeded, having blown in on the breeze from neighbouring meadows, and others would have been transplanted; there was no shortage of replacement plants to take their place in the wild in those days. With plenty of manure to enrich the soil – especially if the cottager kept chickens or a pig – and generations of hard-won knowledge of what it takes to make plants grow, these plots of earth surrounding modest homes began to evolve into what we now think of as typical cottage gardens.

Victorian landscape painters presented a romanticised view of country living, with their pictures of picturesque thatched cottages, half-hidden beneath flowering roses and honeysuckle, with hollyhocks standing sentry by the door. Only rarely did they show the dilapidated cottage interiors, with running damp on the walls and holes in the ceiling. Who can blame them, however? Town-dwellers, both rich and poor, were busy earning a living in newly industrialised Britain, yet they still yearned for the countryside of their forebears.

Apparently Queen Victoria empathised with this point of view. Certainly during her reign a great many towns and cities created public parks, a good number of which are still with us today. Within their boundaries, ordinary people rediscovered the joy of walking amongst meadows, shrubs and trees, or watching their children playing games safely away from traffic. City slums, where even the tiniest garden was an impossible dream, abounded, yet within these parks – often guarded by seemingly fierce Park Keepers – simple pleasures remained.

Nowadays traditional cottage gardens can embellish the exterior of almost any type of home, be it in town or country. Rediscovery of the benefits of organic gardening has helped them flourish. The ingredients include old-fashioned flowers such as pinks, lavender and columbines, and medicinal and culinary herbs like sage, marjoram and mint – often close to the kitchen door. Vegetables are planted higgledy-piggledy, with admirable disregard for conventionality. Rows of scarlet-flowered runner beans twine up rustic sticks amongst marigolds and marguerites, clusters of lettuces plump up in odd gaps, while small but sweet-flavoured tomatoes shine like rubies against sun-warmed walls.

Our ancestors would probably feel more at home nowadays in gardens such as these than they would indoors.

A cottage garden wheelbarrow.

Parasol mushroom.

HAYMAKING

MOWING BY HAND

Early on mid-summer mornings, from the Middle Ages until around the final years of the nineteenth century, farm workers would gather to begin hand-mowing the still dew-laden meadow grass. Each carried a long-handled, sinuous scythe, whose shape differed slightly from one district to another, but always ended in a curved and lethally sharp blade, set

Both muscles and skill are needed for cutting hay by hand.

at right-angles to the handle. These mowers were skilled at their job, and each had a favourite whetstone to keep their blade in top condition.

Farm workers dressed for practicality and comfort. Older men might have worn a smock, that surprisingly strong outer garment with rows of 'smocking stitch' gathering its white or oatmeal-coloured material across the chest. Younger men, meanwhile, wore comfortably loose, collarless shirts, with sleeves rolled up for action. Whether worn beneath a smock or a shirt, however, the men's trousers were designed for comfort.

A countryman's smock.

A broad leather belt held them up, and a length of cord tied beneath each knee stopped field mice, or – more worryingly – rats, running up their trouser legs. Some traditionalists wore 'buskins' – leggings made of canvas or leather that buttoned up the side – above their boots. Straw or felt hats, meanwhile, kept the sun from their heads.

With the mowing team advancing across the meadow in a meandering line, the ripe grass swished softly to earth, to dry in the strengthening sun. Come 11 a.m., the mowers would gather beneath a sturdy tree – left there to give shade to the animals that would later graze this same field – to have their 'dockys' of tea, bread and cheese. While later in the afternoon they would have their 'bever' or 'foursies' – another bottle of cold tea, with more bread and cheese, perhaps brought across by one of their children.

As the day progressed, the old-fashioned grasses, particularly sweet vernal, were mown and their sweet fragrance filled the air. Not all of the meadow flowers had finished blooming by this time – there would have been a succession of flower heads mingling with the growing grass for several months now – and petals fluttered down like confetti at a country wedding. Flower seeds mingled with those of a dozen or so varieties of meadow grasses as they fell to the ground together. As the sun's heat increased, so the seed ripening process accelerated.

The distribution of

Hand-made pitchfork and flail.

A fragrant, fresh-mown meadow.

Swallows favour beams in open barns, while house martins live up to their name and choose house eaves to build their mud nests.

Sand martins are the odd ones out in this family group. As their name implies, they choose sandbanks for their homes; both sexes excavate a tunnel about 30 cms. long, where eggs are laid and their chicks are raised.

Birds of prey, be they kestrel, sparrowhawk, merlin or even peregrine falcon, add a literal dash of excitement to a meadow. With slender, pointed wings (although a sparrowhawk's are broad) and impressive turns of speed – particularly the peregrine, who is reputed to be able to dive at between one hundred and two hundred miles an hour – they cull the weaker birds of other species. The majority of small birds evade them, however, just as many insects evade these same small birds.

When night falls, owls come into their own. Little owls can sometimes be glimpsed during the day, perching stock-still out on a high branch. Tawny owls use this same trick, but lean in close to the tree trunk. Other birds are not slow to spot them, however, due to their bulk. Furious bursts of 'pinking' and scolding often draw the attention of meadow-strolling humans to this spectacle of tiny, feathered 'Davids' attacking a sleepy 'Goliath'.

Short-eared owls are often the first to fly of a late afternoon, their wide golden eyes presenting a startling appearance as they

Hollow trees make good nesting sites for owls.

hunt low over the grass. Barn owls, meanwhile, wait till dusk, before flying like silent white ghosts as the first stars begin to appear in the sky.

You never know what birds will turn up in a meadow – but that's all part of the pleasure. There's one that is almost guaranteed to put in an appearance, however, as soon as you unpack your sandwiches – a robin.

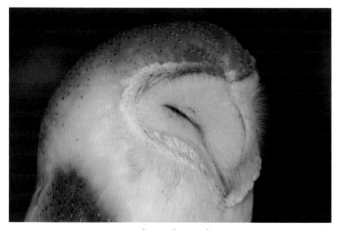

A sleeping barn owl.

BIRDS OF WET MEADOWS

A whooper swan sits calmly on her nest.

Whether they are official watermeadows glinting in slanting rays of winter sun, or simply soggy fields with blocked drains, some birds revel in them. There's no need to name everything that flies, float, preens or dozes before you. It's a treat just to be there and absorb the atmosphere of wildness and natural beauty combined.

Swans are amongst the most noticeable of wetland birds, with their elegant necks and pure white plumage shining out on even the mistiest of days. Mute swans, with their bright orange bills, are familiar to us from local lakes and rivers. Whooper and Bewick swans, meanwhile, have beaks that are a mixture of yellow and black. On the whooper swan's beak, this yellow extends almost to the tip, whilst the Bewick swan – which is the smaller of the two birds – has a mostly black beak, with just a small patch of yellow at the top.

Geese are the next down in size, and similar in shape to swans – although a little more portly. Greylag geese are frequently seen, their orange beak and pink feet setting off a uniformly greyish-brown body. Most other types of geese have darker feathers, plus individual clues to identification. Bean geese, for instance, have an orange and black bill, and orange legs. Pink-footed geese possess a dark head and neck, and pink feet and legs. White-fronted geese, meanwhile, have a narrow white band just above and around their beaks.

Some geese, however, are predominantly black and white, rather than brown. Canada geese are the ones many people see on a semi-regular basis, for they frequent urban lakes just as happily as remote watermeadows. Their long black necks, with a strikingly white chin-strap, make them easy to identify. Barnacle geese are smaller, daintier versions of Canada geese. Their entire face is white, not just the chin. Brent geese are also rather dainty, as geese go, with a light patch at the front of their dark throat.

Ducks are sociable creatures, dabbling together in groups – quacking companionably. Female ducks are generally modestly attired in muted shades of brown, in direct contrast to their showy mates. Shelducks are an exception to that rule, as both sexes are large and impressive, with bottle-green heads, mostly white bodies and broad chestnut breastbands. Mallards are a

A fine pair of mallards.

firm favourite, popping up as they do in almost any watery environment. The male has a green head and chestnut breast, separated by a narrow white collar. Wigeon are attractive ducks, with a chestnut breast and head, with a broad mustard-coloured stripe from beak to crown. Teal are petite but beautiful, possessing a chestnut head, green eye-stripe (with gold edging), plus a distinctive white line above the wing and a buff patch each side of its tail.

Should you see a large grey and white duck with a brown head, and a tail as thin as a hat-pin, that's an aptly named pintail. On the other hand, if you find a portly duck with chestnut flanks, bottle green head and a shovel-shaped bill – that's a shoveler. A little black and white duck with a fetching black tuft on the back of its head is called a tufted duck, and a little black and grey duck with a strikingly chestnut head is called (for no obvious reason) a pochard.

A shoveler duck shovels up a snack.

Great-crested grebes are wonderful performers. Slimmer than ducks, with elegant necks and ear-tufts, these brownish-grey and white birds are prone to suddenly dive beneath the water in pursuit of fish. In spring, however, whether on city lake or countryside flooded meadow, these birds put on a

Canada geese nibble the short waterside grass.

wonderful breeding display – pattering across the water, necks outstretched towards their chosen mate, before subsiding in a flurry of sparkling spray.

Waders, those long-legged and long-billed birds, who naturally enough like wading about in shallow water, are confusingly similar when seen from a distance. Two wading birds appear regularly enough in meadows to warrant a mention, though. Curlew are large, long-legged, speckled brown birds, with a distinctively long and down-curved bill, while snipe are smaller, long-legged, brown-barred birds, with a long straight bill.

Come the summer, the water will have receded significantly, and the bird population of damp meadows will have changed. One bird that is likely to be there year-round, though, is the heron. Standing around a metre tall, on stilt-like legs (or more often just one, with the other tucked up to keep warm), this long-necked and big-bodied grey bird is a treat to watch. A study in patience, a heron will pace cautiously along the water's edge, then stand motionless – gazing steadfastly down. Suddenly, it darts into action with its sinuous neck and long beak, to spear a fish, eel or frog for lunch. Then it flies off on those enormous grey wings, so slowly that it seems to defy gravity, to perch on a tree (a big one, naturally).

No matter what the time of year, there's always something to see in a water meadow.

A heron in flight.

MEADOW ANIMALS

Many wild animals love meadows, but most are wary of human beings, and sometimes of each other. Although this is a challenge for nature-watchers, it makes things even more exciting when you do get a chance to see them.

Bats love hollow trees. Indeed, trees can be crucial to their survival: not only do they provide nesting and roosting sites, but they also host many species of insects – breakfast in bed, you could almost say. Ash, beech, oak and ancient Scots pines are all favourite addresses in the bat world. A hollow tree beside a lake, for example, would suit a colony of Daubenton's bats down to the ground (well, to at least six feet above it, to be more precise).

So having spotted an interesting hollow tree, how can you tell whether bats are in residence? If the wood beneath – or directly around – the hole is darkly stained, this is a good clue. Miniature scratch marks around the hole itself show where bats have clung on with their clawed feet, while tiny droppings consisting of dried insect fragments found on the ground beneath, are an excellent sign too. Simpler, perhaps, is to wait quietly nearby at dawn or dusk and watch for bats flying in and out. It is illegal to harm or disturb bats, or their roosting places. Planning authorities and builders are therefore required to check hollow trees for possible usage by these creatures before undertaking any nearby work.

Despite having had a bad press ever since 'Dracula', bats are in fact soft furred, warm-blooded little mammals, with no animosity towards human beings. They simply wish to be left in peace.

Given that deer are amongst our largest wild animals, they are surprisingly difficult to spot at close quarters. During the day they often seek shelter in woodland, only emerging as dusk begins to fall. Yet in quiet meadows you can sometimes come across them peacefully grazing at any time of day. If you discover springtime hedge or tree branches with their bark frayed off, this is a sign of deer marking their territories or rubbing the 'velvet' from their new antlers.

Fallow deer stand 110 cms high at the shoulder, with white-spotted flanks and a broad spread of antlers. Normally be found in forests, semi-domesticated herds can be seen in some of our larger parkland meadows, where they make a striking sight.

Red deer are impressively large (120 cms tall at the shoulder) with deeply–pronged antlers. They favour high grassland with woods nearby. Although normally silent animals, stags roar impressively in the autumn rut (mating season).

Roe deer are the species most likely to be seen in meadows. Despite measuring only 75 cm at shoulder height, they can jump over hedges and fences with ease, so can pop up in almost

any grassy space. The most frequent view of them, however, is of their white rumps as they gallop away.

Dormice (body 8 cms, twice that length when you include their tail) are often voted amongst the country's favourite wild animals. Sadly now rare, due to diminishing hazel coppices and beech woods, this golden-furred little creature with its shiny black boot-button eyes and long bushy tail is usually only spotted by accident. It's worth looking carefully along meadow hedges thick with hazel, honeysuckle and brambles, however, as these form an ideal habitat. Nibbled hazel shells, with a smooth round hole where the kernel has been extracted, plus an outer ring of neat tooth-marks, are good clues to look for.

Nocturnal by nature, dormice emerge from their domed summer nests of grass, moss and stripped honeysuckle bark, to climb nimbly along slender branches in search of nuts and berries. Occasionally they will take advantage of a bird box as a nesting site, especially if the entrance hole is near to the tree trunk (rather than facing outwards).

In autumn, dormice – plump now from their non-stop nocturnal nibbling – curl up their winter nests (which are nearer the ground, for shelter) and sleep through till late spring. They really need a 'Please do not disturb' notice on their doorways, though, as they are one of our most endangered mammals. Protected by law, these attractive creatures should not be handled without a licence from English Nature.

A country fox (110 cms long, including his bushy tail or 'brush') is less often seen than his urban counterpart, yet when one is spotted, he's likely to be sauntering casually along with an air of, 'What are you humans doing in my meadow?'

The mating season for foxes is January, when the males give short sharp barks that carry clearly on the frosty night air, and vixens scream in reply. Come the following summer, there's the treat of spotting a family of fox cubs playing hide-and-seek in the long grass, their ginger fur glinting in the sunshine.

A fox's earth may, at first glance, resemble a badger sett. However, its acrid scent will give the game away. Like badgers, they follow regular pathways, but these tend to be narrower – due to their smaller paws. (Sometimes, though, they meet up

A fox sits in the sunshine.

on the same track – which can lead to some amusing situations when both creatures sit back on their haunches in surprise).

Whilst town foxes survive mainly by scavenging from dustbins and rubbish tips, the country fox has to work harder for his living, seeking out rats, mice, voles and even worms or beetles. Rabbits provide a welcome boost to their menu, but are far more difficult to catch.

The grass snake is non-venomous, which is good to know –

A grass snake going for a swim.

Roe deer.

BADGERS

Badgers have been present in this country since the end of the last Ice Age. Much like humans, badgers are sociable creatures. They form strong family bonds and live close to each other within their chosen sections of the family sett – a collection of tunnels that may well have been first excavated by their ancestors generations ago, and been amended, extended and regularly cleaned out ever since.

Fresh hay is a treat for these hygiene-conscious animals. On summer evenings, therefore, you may spot a badger ambling cautiously along a hedgerow to check that the coast is clear, before bounding out to collect a bundle of new-mown hay between their front paws. They then go into reverse gear and shuffle backwards to their sett, clutching this golden bounty with their front legs as they go.

As in any family, bickering sometimes occurs. Badgers are built like furry barrage balloons, however, and there is plenty of spare flesh to take the odd nip – although when niggled, they can make a surprising amount of noise for such normally silent creatures.

Male badgers are somewhat Victorian in their manner, holding themselves aloof from the rough and tumble of their cubs, but badger mothers are models of maternal affection and care. Cubs are born in their sett below ground in February, when wind and weather are unpredictable, so often it's not until a sunny day in May that the rumbustious cubs are finally allowed outside by their watchful mum.

Female badgers will sometimes 'baby-sit' each other's cubs, while they take it in turns to seek out earthworms. When the cubs grow big enough to learn to seek food themselves, the mother will take them out relatively early

A badger's long claws make excellent tools for digging.

to show them how it is done. Having located a source of food or water, she will take a little for herself, then stand back and encourage the cubs to discover the delights of foraging for themselves.

The art of slurping worms – in the manner of children sucking up spaghetti – is one that takes time to master. It's obviously worth persevering, though. For a fully-grown badger (at around 90 cm – three feet – in length) gets through a couple of hundred worms a night and can weigh up to 12 kg (two stone).

It might seem that the obvious place to watch badgers is at their sett, an energetically excavated system of burrows set into a quiet hillside, marked by large spoilheaps of loose soil. It will be far better for the badgers, however, if you can resist this temptation – to avoid frightening them or drawing the attention of others who have less than kindly intentions.

A better alternative is to follow a badger track (a flattened pathway about 10 cm/4 inches wide) that starts from near their sett, until it leads you to a suitable spot.

Then you can return at dusk and wait quietly to see if badgers are in the area.

To have a really good chance of an evening's badger-watching, however, contact your local Badger Trust (also known as Badger Protection Group) or County Wildlife Trust, and ask if you can join one of their wildlife-watching expeditions. Badgers are such delightful animals that it really is worth making the effort.

There have been polarised points of view recently, on the possibility of badgers infecting cattle with Bovine Tuberculosis. When a farmer's livelihood depends on healthy cattle, it is perhaps an understandable reaction to call for the killing of any wild animals that might also be susceptible to the disease. However, government scientists have been slaughtering badgers under licence for many years now, yet are no nearer conclusively proving that badgers are the cause of T.B. in cattle. Indeed, logic dictates that the reverse could be true, with the droppings of sick cattle infecting the pastures that badgers nightly forage for worms.

Some badger setts have caused difficulties when new housing estates have enclosed traditional badger territories. Police have been called when badgers have dug their way beneath garden fences and peppered suburban lawns with 'snuffle holes' in a desperate search for worms. However, Local Police Wildlife Liaison Officers and Badger Trust representatives are happy to visit and advise on any difficulties and it is encouraging to note that local Badger Trusts receive more calls from the general public asking how they can attract badgers into their gardens, rather than asking how to evict them.

If you do indeed live near a badger sett and would like to encourage badgers to linger in your garden – and your neighbours do not possess fierce dogs or pristine lawns – then it is worth experimenting a little. You stand a good chance of gradually enticing them within sight of your home by sprinkling some unsalted peanuts, sultanas and a few drops of honey left out near their regular route each night.

A word of caution, however – please do not try to hand-tame your local badgers – as not all humans are so kindly disposed. We've been leaving food out for local badgers for about fifteen years now. If I'm late delivering their rations, however, and they happen to trundle through the hedgerow just as I'm pouring out some sultanas – they skedaddle! Which is how it should be.

When they reappear, maybe half-an-hour later, as long as we are out of sight in our garden shed, the badgers are perfectly happy to munch, whilst we watch them from the window.

A log scraped by a badger searching for beetles.

since it can grow up to a metre long. However, despite its name this creature prefers to spend its time seeking frogs and newts in the wetter areas of water meadows that humans tend to avoid (for fear of losing their wellingtons). These slender, greenish-bronze reptiles, with their distinctive yellow and black neck rings, appear to enjoy nothing better than zig-zagging through pools of limpid water.

When they are on home territory, hares (65 cms in length) are more extrovert than rabbits, their smaller cousins. In downland meadows on misty spring mornings, males will leap and joust with their rivals – hence the time-honoured phrase, 'Mad as a March hare'. It's fair to say that hares invented kick-boxing long before humans took it up as a sport.

Living above ground as they do, with just a shallow depression in the grass for a nest or 'form', hares need their famous turn of speed to escape hunting foxes or dogs. Streams and ditches seem to slow them not at all – Olympic athletes, every one. If you should spot one whilst it is stationary, however, and some distance away, so that it is hard to distinguish from a rabbit, look for the black tips to its long ears, which mark it out as a hare.

Hedgehogs (average 20 cms from mobile nose to tiny tail) have long been enthusiasts of meadow hedgerows. Nocturnal by nature, a hedgehog can be startlingly noisy if you happen to be strolling through a meadow early in the morning when it is tucking into a large earthworm for breakfast, with enthusiastic snuffles and grunts.

Slugs are another favourite food. (Many gardeners are grateful for hedgehog allies, and are therefore happy to leave an undisturbed corner for this helpful animal's summer nest and winter hibernation spot). Snails are a particularly tasty treat – well, the Romans thought so, anyway – but hedgehogs have to compete with song thrushes to find them.

Thankfully for the mother, baby hedgehogs are born with their embryo spines covered by a layer of skin which resembles 'goose-pimples'; these pop through as the infants grow, gradually changing in colour from white to brown. Older family groups forage companionably together of an evening, until the youngsters can manage on their own.

Lizards (average length 12 cm) are cold-blooded creatures, and as a result take every opportunity to bask in the sun. This is a helpful habit for wildlife watchers, since a quiet approach to a sun-warmed gate, tree-stump or hedge-base may well be rewarded by excellent views of these normally quicksilver reptiles.

Varying in colour from polished pewter to bronze (although on rainy days they look much duller – but don't we all), lizards stalk and catch worms, grubs, insects and spiders, while they in their turn are preyed upon by foxes, snakes and crows. They have adapted to this situation by developing a long tail that will break off if seized – when their tail regrows, the join still shows. These shy and retiring reptiles are entirely harmless to humans.

Infant lizards emerge from their eggs directly they are laid, and begin fending for themselves immediately. They grow quickly, and slough off their old skins at regular intervals, leaving each one like the fragile finger of a glove.

Moles (average length 14 cms) enjoy tunnelling through the soft soil of damp meadows in search of worms. Helped by their pink, shovel-shaped front feet and sensitive whiskers, each mole feels its way along this private underground world. Although it will of course gobble up any worms it comes across during these excavations, every mole needs to regularly patrol its own network of corridors, seeking creatures that have fallen in.

The molehills that mark their underground progress are usually of uniform size and set in curving rows. Occasionally, however, a particularly large central mound is created. Beneath this 'fortress' is a nest, where the naked young are born. As soon as they become independent, however, each young mole disperses to patter along its own tunnel system through life – neatly clad in black velvet.

Wood mice (body 11 cms, tail likewise) patter about hedgerows and meadows, constantly on the alert. Attractive to look at, these small furry creatures possess large eyes and ears, a quivering nose on a honey-brown body, plus their long tail. Despite their name, wood mice are very wide-ranging in their choice of home. At dawn and dusk, they make regular forays through the undergrowth in search of food, returning to their

A harvest mouse hides in a meadow.

Otters seem much larger on land.

nest of grass and leaves from time to time to stock up the larder.

Field (or harvest) mice (7.5 cm body, with a tail virtually the same length), are Europe's smallest variety of mouse. Agile climbers of cornstalks and long grass, they weave domed summer nests amongst the tall stems in which to bring up their young. Although more often pictured amongst fields of wheat or barley, these tiny mice love ungrazed meadows which are cut only once a year, so flower meadows can be a lifeline.

Otters are truly impressive animals, which are making a welcome return to water meadow habitats. Viewed at close quarters, they seem much larger than they appear on the television screen. In reality, an otter measures up to 125 cms from its nose to the tip of its powerful tail, and can gallop towards the water at high speed.

A deep cavity washed out by flood tides beneath the roots of a riverside tree makes an ideal home (or holt) for these impressive chocolate-coloured animals, although they are prepared to travel overland if need be. Water is their true element, however. Here they dive, twist and spiral for the joy of living (and catching fish).

Clues to their presence are partly-eaten fish by the riverside, and a well-used muddy slide down the bank from a riverside meadow to the water. After their sad decline – caused first by hunting, but more recently by water pollution – otters are thankfully now beginning to reappear in their old haunts.

Rabbits (averaging 38 cms in length), though so familiar to us today, were in fact introduced by the Normans after 1066 as a readily-managed source of meat. Kept in warrens and regarded as a valuable asset because of their furry skins and delicate meat, they were guarded from predators (both wild and human).

Nowadays rabbits are a relatively common sight, although myxomatosis significantly depleted their numbers in the 1950s. They usually choose a well-drained, sloping site for their communal warren, with sandy soil being particularly preferred, as it is easy to excavate. Meadows offer rabbits a wide range of nutritious grasses, herbs and wild flowers.

A young rabbit.

Bronze-skinned slow-worms (up to 50 cms long) are neither slow nor worms, and nor are they snakes, although they do superficially resemble them. Classified as legless lizards, their young are born in a transparent membrane – from which they emerge as perfectly formed miniature versions of their parents. Weaving from side to side, adult slow-worms silently approach slugs, worms and snails to devour them with apparent relish. Their young, meanwhile, start with more modest fare – small insects.

Although their menu might be considered uninviting, slow-worms are fascinating to observe going quietly about their business – or curled up like Bronze Age bangles. Harmless and retiring by nature, they spend their spare time sheltering beneath flat stones.

Shrews come in several varieties, all of which are distinguished by long, pointed snouts.

Common shrews are a plump 7.5 cms long, with a tail of half that length. They like to set up home along the base of meadow hedgerows, where their chocolate brown back and pale underside blend into the dappled shade. From here they set out, busily hunting for insects, spiders, beetles, in fact anything small and edible that scuttles across their path.

Pygmy shrews, neatly clad in grey fur, are minute – measuring only 6 cms long, plus a furry tail of two-thirds that length, so they are easily identifiable. They travel through the grassy undergrowth at a smart pace, seeking out small beetles and woodlice.

The water shrew is the portliest member of the shrew family. Its body length is 9 cms with the tail adding another 7 cms. This charming little animal's smoothly-furred body is almost black above and light below, but takes on a silver sheen all over when in the water, due to a coating of trapped air bubbles. Water shrews are also equipped with relatively large feet, which are a great aid for swimming.

Stoats and weasels are closely related furry brown mammals that share a strong family resemblance. Both are short-legged and long bodied, and they hunt by running along the ground in search of voles and mice. They are also quite capable of tackling rabbits, which folklore states they hypnotise by twirling in circles in front of their victim.

The stoat is the larger of the two, measuring some 37 cms from its snub nose to the end of its long, black-tipped tail. Its fur is brown above and creamy white below. When in a hurry, stoats bound along energetically.

A weasel on the lookout.

Chestnut-backed weasels are just 25 cms. in length, and correspondingly slimmer than their brown cousins, but they use this to their advantage when pursuing prey down narrow tunnels. They appear to flow through grass in a sinuous motion that is strangely fascinating.

Squirrels are drawn to meadows because of their hedgerow trees. Hedgerows allow the trees dotted along them space to spread their branches fully towards the sun without being overshadowed, thus providing squirrels with bumper crops of seeds, nuts and acorns.

Red squirrels (body 25 cms, tail 20 cms) with their auburn fur and tufted ears, are largely confined to wilder outskirts of the country these days, where they feast daintily on pinecones.

The grey squirrels (body 30 cms, tail 24 cms) that have colonised most other areas have their own special appeal, however. Bold by nature, they are happy to take advantage of food provided by humans. Peanuts are their particular favourite, so if you are putting these out for wild birds, you will need a metal, nibble-proof dispenser.

Both red and grey squirrels construct dreys of leaves, grass and moss, high amongst the strongest branches of trees, where their young are born. Come winter, these same dreys are given a further layer of insulation and used for hibernation – although whenever a mild spell arrives, squirrels clamber down to earth in search of their buried stores of food.

Three varieties of voles pop up in meadows from time to time, and can be distinguished from mice by their rounded muzzles and plump appearance:

Bank voles are covered in brown fur, and measure 10 cms in body length, plus 6 cms of tail. They dwell in grassy banks and verges. Apparently short-sighted, they are not unduly put out by the presence of humans. They follow a mainly vegetarian diet of fruit and seeds, but will devour an insect by way of a change.

Field voles (body 13 cms, tail 4.5 cms) have somewhat longer, greyish fur and love grassland. They potter along their own series of semi-open tunnels, nibbling leaves and juicy stems in passing.

Water voles (body 20 cms, tail 10 cms) are rare these days, being vulnerable to water pollution. However, give it a healthy stream flowing through a meadow, and this plump little vegetarian – famously mis-named as 'Ratty' in *The Wind in the Willows* – is literally in its element.

MEADOW FLOWERS

Bright yellow fleabane brightens an autumn meadow.

Why are people so fond of wild flowers? Could it be that the answer is the same as when a famous mountaineer was asked why he climbed mountains? "Because they're there!"? Whilst wild flowers make us feel good even if we do not know their names, distinguishing one from another can be an enjoyable pastime, so here are a few pointers to some of our more familiar meadow flowers.

Average heights are shown as: Tall = over 30 cms high, Medium = between 15–30 cms high, Small = less than 15 cms high.

YELLOW FLOWERS

Agrimony (T) flaunts spires of single yellow blooms in dry meadows, while meadow rue (T) prefers damp meadows to display its multi-bloomed floral spires. Dyer's greenweed (T) meanwhile, has floppier soft-stemmed spires of blooms. Toadflax (T) looks like a dainty yellow snapdragon as it brightens grassy slopes.

The dandelion-related autumn hawkbit (T) has smaller flowers on taller stems in late summer, while catsear (T) has furry round-tipped leaves and hawksbeard (T) has several small flowerheads on branched stems. Goatsbeard (T) has a large, single yellow flower on a tall stem. This flower closes up its petals at midday – hence its nickname 'Jack-go-to-bed-at-noon'.

Birdsfoot trefoil (S) has bright yellow blooms and clover-like leaves, while lesser trefoil (S) actually resembles yellow clover.

Buttercups are meadow favourites. Bulbous buttercup (M) hides down-turned sepals beneath its golden petals and prefers lime soil, but otherwise resembles its more familiar cousin the meadow buttercup. Marsh marigolds or kingcups (T) are king-size, golden-cupped versions of buttercups, which love riverside meadows.

Cowslip (S) display clusters of bright yellow trumpet flowers and wild daffodil (M) found in meadows are smaller versions of their garden daffodil cousins.

Fleabane (T) is a distinctive bright yellow, daisy-like flower, with several flower heads to each crinkly-leaved stem. While yellow rattle (M) has small yellow trumpet flowers, emerging from green sheaths, which dry to brown in mid-summer.

Toadflax.

Grey squirrels' inquisitiveness helps them to flourish.

A field of snakeshead fritillaries.

PINK, MAUVE AND PURPLE FLOWERS

Some meadows have clumps of tall flowers. Knapweed (T), for instance, has dark pink, thistle-like flowerheads, on tall but thorn-free stems. Marjoram (T), meanwhile, has clusters of small-petalled, mauve flowerheads and prefers lime soils. Damp meadows may contain water mint (T), which has aromatic clusters of pinky-mauve flowers growing up a central stem. Ragged robin (T) – with its slenderly cut pink petals – also flourishes in damp meadows, while red campion (T), with notched pink petals, flourishes in dry ones.

The somewhat shorter milkmaids, cuckoo flower or lady's smock (M) – choose your favourite name – sport slender clusters of pink-mauve blooms, which tremble as spring breezes ripple through the meadow grass. Red clover (M), on the other hand, is a sturdy plant, spreading out into colourful mats of leaves and bloom. Bright pink centaury blooms (S) are small but perky little stars.

Snakeshead fritillaries (M-T) are rare, but found in some water meadows; they have cupped, purple (or occasionally white) chequered blooms that dangle from slender stems.

Orchids are another meadow bonus. Bee orchids (S-M) are pink, with a brown centre resembling a bee, and unspotted leaves. Common spotted orchids (S-M) have pinkish-purple (or occasionally white) flowers, with leaves that are spotted dark purple. Fragrant orchids (S-M) have pinkish-purple blooms that are faintly fragrant, and unspotted leaves.

Marsh orchids come in early, northern and southern varieties. Flowers on all of them vary in height according to the fertility of their soil, and their flowers can range from white to pink or purple. The all share plain green leaves. The pyramidal orchid (S-M) has a pink, conical flowerhead and unspotted leaves.

Pyramidal orchid.

Bee orchid and quaking grass.